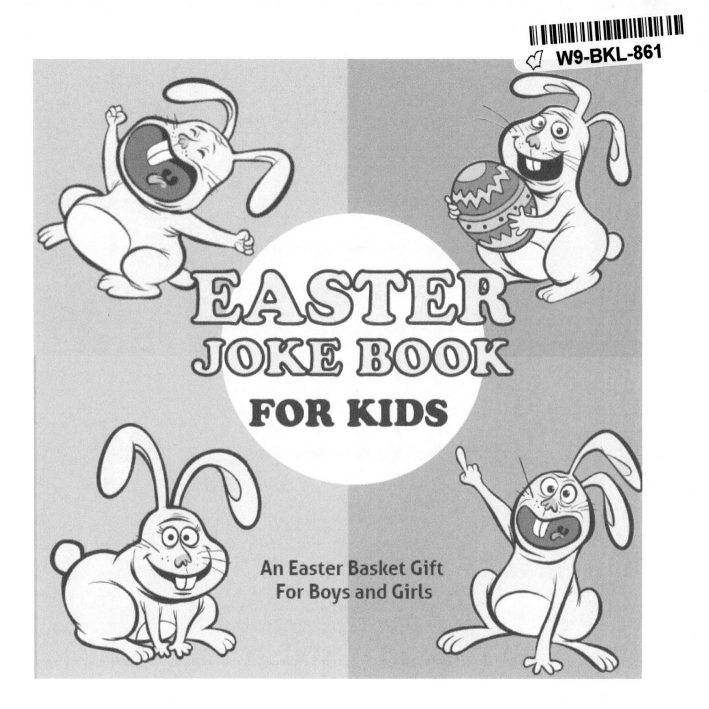

EASTER
JOKE BOOK
FOR KIDS

An Easter Basket Gift
For Boys and Girls

WHAT IS THE "TRY NOT TO LAUGH CHALLENGE"?

For those unfamiliar with this recently popular game, the concept is you tell jokes that are so bad...so groan-worthy...such...dad jokes... that they actually can be funny. However, that's not what makes it a game. So why is the word "challenge" in the name?

It's all about the delivery!

The jokes are interchangeable, but the person telling it is where the magic's at. It's a game of skill of making the other person laugh because of impeccable delivery and timing and emphasis on the right words. Likewise, it's steeling yourself against an opponent's keen delivery.

HOW TO PLAY

1. There are 2 players at a time.
2. Decide who is the "Joker Teller" first. The other person is the "listener"
3. The "joke teller" can pick any joke at random from the book and tell ONE joke.
4. After the joke is told, the book switches hands, and the "joke teller" becomes the "listener", and back and forth after each joke.
5. There is no limit to how many times a joke can be used, but cannot be used back-to-back. You (as the Joker Teller) have to choose at least one different joke in between on your turns.
6. NO CHEATING! When we say "AT RANDOM" we mean it. It's no fun if someone reads all the jokes and knows the punchlines.

SCORING

7. If the other person, the "Listener", laughs, giggles, guffaws, or chortles...even a little bit...the "Joke Teller" gets 1 point.
8. Smiles and smirks and grins do NOT count as points. It must be audible, even if quiet.
9. The first person to get 3 points is the winner!

Why shouldn't you tell jokes to Easter eggs?

They might crack up

What did the snowman ask the other snowman?

Do you smell carrots?

What happened when the Easter Bunny got in trouble at school?

He was eggspelled

How many Easter eggs fit in an empty basket?

One. After that it's not empty anymore

Have you heard the joke about the butter?

I better not tell you...it might spread.

Why did the cabbage finish the race before the bunny?

Because it was a-head

Why was the Easter Bunny wearing a hat?
He was having a bad hare day.

What's the difference between a fish and a guitar?
You can't tuna fish.

How do you know that carrots are good for your eyesight?

Have you ever seen a rabbit wearing glasses?

Where does the Easter Bunny like to go for breakfast?

IHOP

Why do ducks have tail feathers?

To cover their butt-quacks.

What do you get from an overly pampered cow?

Spoiled milk.

What do you call a bunny with fleas?

Bugs Bunny

What is the Easter Bunny's favorite kind of music?

Hip Hop

Why is Easter a good day to go to the beach?

Because it's on Sunday

Why doesn't the Easter Bunny bring Elsa a balloon in her basket?

Because she will let it go.

How does the Easter Bunny dry off after a shower?

With a hare dryer

What do you call an Easter egg that plays tricks on people?

A practical yolker

WHAT DID THE RABBIT SAY TO THE DOG?

NOTHING, RABBITS CAN'T TALK,

HOW DOES THE EASTER BUNNY STYLE ITS FUR?

WITH HARE SPRAY

What bow can't be tied into a knot?

Rainbows

How can you tell which is the oldest rabbit?

Just look for the gray hares

What is the Easter Bunny's favorite sport?

Basket-ball

What do you call a sleepy Easter egg?

Eggs-austed

WHAT DOES AN EVIL HEN LAY?

DEVILED EGGS

WHY ARE FROGS SO HAPPY?

THEY EAT WHATEVER BUGS THEM

Why was Peter Cottontail hopping down the bunny trail?

Because he still too young to drive

What if the Easter Bunny's nose was 12 inches long?

It would be a foot

What kind of vegetable always seems angry?

A steamed carrot

I wanted to tell you a joke about an egg...

...but it's not all it's cracked up to be.

How can the Easter Bunny talk to giants?

He uses big words

What do you call an alien Easter egg?

Egg-stra terrestrial

What do you get when you cross a cow and a duck?

Cheese and quackers

Why did the Easter egg hide?

He was a little chicken.

What dog keeps the best time?

A watch dog.

What season is it when you are on a trampoline?

Spring time.

What do you call a rabbit without an eye?

A rabbt.

Why doesn't the bunny have giraffes in her class?

Because giraffes are all in High school

Why do bees have sticky hair?

They use honeycombs.

Where does the Easter Bunny go when he needs a new tail?

To a re-tail store

How does the Easter Bunny like to travel?

By hare-plane

Why do you never see the Easter Bunny hiding in a tree?

Because he is so good at it

Why did the bird have to go to the hospital?

It needed a tweet-ment.

What kind of jewelry does the Easter Bunny wear?

14 Carrot Gold

Where does Valentine's Day come after Easter?

In the dictionary

Why do chocolate bunnies look sad?

They always feel hollow inside.

Why did the bunny cross the road?

It was the chicken's day off.

What has ears but can't hear?

A cornfield.

Why did the Easter Bunny eat his homework?

Because the teacher told him it was a piece of cake

Where would you find your rabbit?

The same place you lost it.

When is the best time to go to the dentist?

At tooth-hurty

Why don't rabbits chew gum?

They do, just not in public

What kind of stories does the Easter Bunny like?

The ones with hoppy endings

Why couldn't the bunny see the movie about pirates?

It was rated Arrrrrrr

WHAT DO YOU CALL A FUNNY MOUNTAIN?

HILL-ARIOUS

WHY THE DID THE BUNNY CROSS THE PLAYGROUND?

TO GET TO THE OTHER SLIDE

What do you call a line of rabbits jumping backwards?

A receding hare-line

What kind of lights did Noah use on the Ark?

Flood lights

Why did the mommy rabbit go to the barber?

She had a lot of little hares.

How does the Easter Bunny stay in shape?

Eggs-ercise

Why did the cookie go to the hospital?

He felt crumb-y

Why are eggs afraid to go down dark alleys?

They don't want to get beat up

What did the triangle say to the circle?
Your pointless

Why can't the duck help the Easter Bunny?
Because he kept quacking the eggs

Why did the rabbit throw the clock out of the window?

Because he wanted to see time fly.

Why did the teddy bear say no to dessert?

Because she was stuffed

How did the Easter Bunny grow his ears?

From Eggplants.

How do rabbits stay cool in the summertime?

Hare conditioning

What do you call a cross between a toad with a rabbit?

A bunny ribbit.

What do you call a rich bunny?

A billion-hare.

WHERE DID THE RABBIT GO SKIING?

AT THE BUNNY HILL.

WHAT DID THE BUNNY SAY TO HIS CARROT?

BEEN NICE GNAWING YOU

Q. What do rabbits have that nothing else can?

A. Baby rabbits

How many rabbits does it take to change a light bulb?

One, but only if it hops right to it.

What kind of story books do bunnies like best?

Ones with hoppy endings.

How do you catch a unique bunny rabbit?

Unique up on it.

How do you know carrots are good for your eyes?

You never see rabbit's wearing eye-glasses.

What is a rabbit's favorite kind of dance?

Hip-Hop

WHERE DO RABBITS GO AFTER THEY GET MARRIED?

ON THEIR BUNNYMOON!

WHAT DO YOU CALL A RABBIT WHO IS ANGRY BECAUSE HE GOT BURNED?

A HOT CROSS BUNNY

Why are rabbits lucky?

They have four rabbit's feet

What do you call a rabbit wearing a kilt?

Hopscotch.

What was the name of the bank robber rabbits?

Bunny and Clyde.

How many hairs are there in a rabbit's tail?

None! The hairs are all on the outside.

What do you get when a rabbit is with Winnie the Pooh?

A honey bunny.

What did the rabbit use to propose to his girlfriend?

A 14-carrot ring

What do rabbits put in a computer?

A hoppy disk

What do rabbits sing at birthday parties?

Hoppy birthday to you!

How do rabbits like to travel?

By hareplane.

What do rabbits say before dinner?

Lettuce pray.

WHAT IS A BUNNY'S MOTTO?

DON'T WORRY, BE HOPPY!

HOW ARE RABBITS LIKE CORN STALKS?

THEY BOTH HAVE BIG EARS.

Why did the bunny say about the scary movie?

It was hare-raising

What do you call a rabbit with the sniffles?

A runny bunny!

Why does Peter Cottontail hop down the bunny trail?

He is too young to drive!

How does a rabbit throw a tantrum?

He gets hopping mad!

BONUS!

10 Easter themed coloring pages!

Made in the USA
Monee, IL
21 March 2020